DAYS IN DEVONPORT
Part V

Gerald W. Barker

Growth of Civic Spirit

There were great rejoicings in Devonport on the receipt of Sir Robert Peel's letter in December, 1823, conveying the King's pleasure that on and after 1st January, 1824, the town of Plymouth Dock should be known as Devonport. There were proclamations and fanfares of trumpets, processions and bands, banquets and free toasts, liberal entertainment for the poor and lavish decoration of the streets with arches and flags. A commemorative medal was struck, and on 12th August, 1824, the King's birthday, the foundation stone of the 125 ft. Greek doric column, designed by John Foulston, was laid. The granite tower was completed the following year, without however, the proposed statue of King George IV adorning the top. The cost of nearly £3,000 was raised by public subscription. Devonport was eventually amalgamated with Plymouth and Stonehouse in 1914.

This version of the book is virtually as originally published, presenting the work of Gerald W Barker. There are now additional pages at the back providing information about the publisher, Arthur L Clamp.

The republishing project is being managed by Arthur's grandson, Steven Gibson. We aim to find all the research that he was involved in publishing, preserving it for the next generation as part of 'The Clamp Collection'.

INTRODUCTION

WHO was the naval officer whose visit to the Devonport Hospital was to be shrouded in secrecy? Only two men on the hospital staff knew his identity, one of whom was Admiral Lawrence W. Braithwaite, Chairman of the hospital, and Mr. F. E. Pine, its administrator. The war at the time in the early 1940s had been going badly for Great Britain.

The Royal Navy had a long association with the hospital. It helped not only in financial terms in the days before the National Health Service but in many other supportive ways.

Before the building of the hospital in 1862 there existed in Devonport a Public Dispensary in a building in Chapel Street that was later used as the Parochial Office. The growth of the Dockyard Borough, however, made it necessary for those interested in the health of the inhabitants to consider the question of improved facilities. Plans were prepared by the Architect, Mr. Alfred Norman of Devonport, and the building was commenced in March, 1862. On 1st December, 1863, the hospital was opened when ten beds became available for the reception of general patients. The Emma Ward for children (18 beds) was ready in 1865. The Admiralty, who maintained the Lock Wards, increased the beds in 1867 from 62 to 162.

The first President of the new hospital was Major General W. N. Hutchinson, Lieutenant Governor of Plymouth. Amongst the first Life Governors were; The Prince of Wales (afterwards King Edward VII), The Earl Fortescue, The Earls of Mount Edgcumbe and St. Germans, Lord Clinton, T.G., Agar Roberts Esq., M.P. and Edward St. Aubyn, esq. No less than 26 of the 63 Presidents who were elected during the period 1863-1934 were directly connected with either the army or navy.

The portion of the building devoted to the treatment of venereal disease was closed on the 1st May, 1903, and taken over by the Admiralty by whom it was used during the 1914-1918 War as a hospital, and then retained by them as a War College and Port Library.

During the First World War the serious falling off in revenue menaced the very existence of the hospital. In 1918 a special meeting of the Governors was summoned to consider the situation. A proposal to close the hospital until such time as accumulated funds should justify its reopening was submitted. It was recognised it would, however, be a disaster to the people of Devonport and it was decided to form a special committee to formulate schemes for the purpose of placing the hospital on a sound financial position. Investments were few and the hospital dependant upon voluntary contributions for its maintenance; it had relied over many years on supplementing its income by obtaining voluntary contributions from the workers in the area. The Hospital Sunday and Alexandra Rose Day Funds were other sources of income.

The Penny-in-the-Pound Scheme started in 1923. In 1930 it was decided at a meeting of the Governors and Subscribers of the Three Voluntary Hospitals of the city viz., The South Devon and East Cornwall Hospital (Greenbank) and the Central Hospital (Lockyer Street) and the Royal Albert Hospital to join the unification scheme.

On 12th July, 1934, The Prince of Wales' Hospital Plymouth Act received the Royal Assent and the Voluntary Hospitals of Plymouth entered upon a new era. The outbreak of war in 1939 saw additional beds set up under the Emergency Hospital Service. Arrangements for dealing with air raid casualties were made. These arrangements were put to practical test on a number of occasions and ensured prompt and effective treatment for the victims of enemy action. Mr. Slee, the Marlborough Street butcher, who was killed by his shop receiving a direct hit by a bomb, was taken to the hospital mortuary.

The Royal Naval Officer, who came to the Port Library at the hospital under a cloak of secrecy was Captain "D" (Lord Louis Mountbatten). His ship, H.M.S. *Javelin* was torpedoed in November, 1940, and had to be towed into Devonport. Mr. F. E. Pine had to ensure that a room was made available for the developing of film, in connection with war operations, in an annexe adjacent to the Port Library, without the rest of the hospital staff becoming aware of it.

On 5th July, 1948, transfer of the hospitals to the Ministry of Health brought about many changes. The first year of the National Health Service passed with less difficulty than anticipated.

In its centenary year 1963 the hospital changed its title to that of the Devonport section of the Plymouth General Hospital but still continued to be known to the residents of Devonport with affection as the "Royal Albert".

Acknowledgements

My special thanks to Mr. F. E. Pine, Administrator of Devonport Hospital and Mr. L. Presland, X-Ray Department of Derriford Hospital for all their help with photographs and information of Devonport Hospital. For the photo of Portland Place reproduced by the Photograph Department of H.M. Naval Base. Also to Mr. R. Rundell, Secretary of the Hertfordshire Postcard Club, Mr. G. Fleming, Mrs. J. R. Gribbell, Mr. R. Watkins, Miss L. M. Hooper, Mr. P. F. Ghillyer, Mr. J. Williams, Mr. H. Feabes, Mr. R. Smith, Mrs. C. Gardner, Mr. A. C. Barker, Mr. R. Blazier, Mr. R. Burgoyne, Mrs. M. Laxton, Mr. C. Hambly, Mr. F. J. Boase, Mrs. J. Pengelly, Mr. D. Cloake, Mr. R. Glover, Mrs. B. Hearn, Mrs. B. Glanville, Mr. G. Bickle, Mrs. I. Fryer, Mrs. N. Pollard, Mr. A. Rickard, Mr. J. Prance, Mrs. K. Smeaton and to Arthur L. Clamp who, when "stalking" around Devonport with his camera, took the last shot of the hospital's gold lettering, see page 5. There will be more photographs of the hospital in book 6.

Gerald W. Barker,
44 Burnham Park Road,
Peverell, Plymouth.

Appendix

World War II should read World War I, page 16, book 4.

Solly Stephens "house" should be "shop", page 17, book 4.

Carnival 1928

Putty Philpotts is the Carnival King and Edith Mayne the Queen. The much loved Harry Harcourt, manager of the *Tivoli* Picture House is on the left. He would dress up as a circus clown and join in the procession to help to raise money for the hospital. He received loud cheers from the people lining both sides of the streets. He was the poor man's friend and the unemployeds' "Patron Saint". Like so many others he gave willingly of his time to help the Royal Albert Hospital, supported entirely by voluntary contributions. The Matron, Miss A. Kenwell, is standing with the group.

Granby Barracks to Starboard!

The photograph taken from the Royal Fleet Club shows the gate leading into the Granby Army Barracks on the extreme right. The lodge is on the left of the main entrance. Mr. Percy Hunt was one of the Keepers. The late Pat Mowan, noted local historian, lived in the Gate Lodge with his parents for many years. To the left of the lodge is No. 3 Station, which had its own ambulance and where the voluntary St Johns crew slept. The Gas Decontamination Centre is to the left of the Nurses Home (built in 1899). The rectangular board states: *SOUTH DEVON EAST CORNWALL HOSPITAL DEVONPORT.* (It was so named in 1948).

War College Room
One of the rooms of the Royal Naval War College contained large tables. During "manoeuvres" the model warships on the tables would be moved by the use of long wooden sticks. The board to the right of the word *NORTH* contained the names of ships and "sinkings". The large tables in this room, which eventually became the Washbourn Ward in 1973, when the Admiralty returned it to the Hospital, were reduced in size in 1939 to enable the room to be converted into offices.

1928
On the left is the radiographer Frank Rowe. Mr. George Wherry, the Hospital Secretary is on the right, and the nurse is Mary Beaton. From the lower part of the civilian section ran a passage leading to the Royal Naval section. No civilian could enter the naval section without permission of the Captain of the Port Library.

1978
Fifty years on. In bed is Out Patient Nurse Mitchell. Standing by the bed is Mrs. Shirley Williams, dark room assistant. On the left is radiographer Mr. Les Presland and on the right is Mr. Edwin Pine, Hospital Secretary. These two gentlemen have worked hard over the years to preserve the historical records of the hospital.

The Public Ceremony

The weather during March onwards in 1862 was very unfavourable. The public ceremony was postponed until the erection of the building had advanced to the stage of receiving the memorial stone, and that it should be laid with masonic honours. This was done on the 17th June, 1862. The Earl of Mount Edgcumbe agreed to perform the office. The Devonport Rifle Volunteers attended in full dress as a guard of honour. Freemasons appeared carrying the regalia and flags belonging to the order.

One Hour To Go

On the Devonport Park side of the Hospital could be seen in gold lettering: *ROYAL ALBERT HOSPITAL SUPPORTED BY VOLUNTARY CONTRIBUTIONS*. Mr. Arthur L. Clamp, local historian, photographed this picture within one hour of its demolition. The Victorian building, with its limestone walls peppered with shrapnel, survived the blitz. It will long be cherished in the memory as an edifice of loving care for all its patients.

Through Cholera and Smallpox

Four years before Mr. Thomas Woollcombe died there was a smallpox epidemic. A plaque in the hospital chapel, which was near the nurses home, was erected to the memory of Dr. John Wilson, M.D. M.R.C.S. He was a junior surgeon who died from the effects of a poison wound received in the execution of his duty in the epidemic of 1872. Mr. J. C. Sullivan's (he now lives in West Park) mother remembers the smallpox ships in the Sound in the 1890s. She knew one of the lady volunteers that went to help.

The Devonport Alhambra Theatre

TAVISTOCK STREET.

Proprietors — THE PROVINCIAL THEATRES SYNDICATE, LTD.
Managing Director — MR. JACK GLADWIN.
Resident Manager — Mr. W. ELLYTHORNE FRASER.

'Phone—Devonport 385.

May 14th 1932

To whom it may concern.

Mr. Clarence Hambley has been employed at the above for eight years, first as stage manager & electrician, & for the last two years as chief operator.

During that period we have always found him to be efficient, conscientious, willing & obliging, & are pleased to recommend him.

W. Ellythorne Fraser
Manager

Devonport's Theatres

Clarry Hambly was stage manager from the time of the opening of the *Alhambra Theatre* 1924 as a stock company till 1932 when it closed temporarily owing to competition. He remembers it going over to talkies in 1929. Fitted by R.C.A. Photophone Ltd., one of the only two American Companies engaged in talkie equipment. Clarry, with two others, took one week working night and day, never leaving the building to help with installation. Mr. Hambly was the Chief Operator. The *Alhambra* didn't have any silent films. They started with an American Spectacular called, *Whoopee!* Competition, however, with the *Grand* and *Savoy* in Union Street, who had "first runs", was too fierce and so the *Alhambra* closed in 1932. It opened again six months later under Mr. Rice with Music Hall Vaudeville Shows.

Mrs. Frances McTighe Remembers

The *Stein Song* will never be forgotten. As a child I lived in Cross Street, which was at the back of the *Alhambra* in line with the stagedoor. In 1929 the song was played continuously throughout the night as preparations were made to introduce sound films into the theatre. The lights outside the stagedoor shone right into the bedroom. We children loved it, but our parents weren't amused at being kept awake. Talking to the chorus girls through their dressing room window was a happy experience. Some would open their window so that we could watch them putting on their make-up. Some of them invited me to have tea with them at their "digs" in Princess Street, Devonport. We had cherries and cream, which was a luxury, as I was one of a large family. They also gave me a silk handkerchief.

I remember the Dorothy Mullard shows, mostly dramatic. Also I recall *"The Cat* and *The Canary"* and *"Sweeney Todd"*. The villains were a husband and wife team called Herbert Evelyn and Millie Phillips. The comedians were Billy and Kitty Owen, and the heroine was Valerie Crispin. Mrs. McTighe, whose maiden name was Harding, remembers making friends with the actors and actresses. Herbert and Millie visited her stepsister's (Kathleen Poole) birthday party and invited her back to the theatre's dressing room. The film projectionist's name was Arthur Johnson, who lived at Torpoint. Mrs. McTighe's boy friend Roy, a bell-bottomed sailor, was in later years standing on her door step, when Ivy Benson and her band of girls walked by. Each one touched his naval collar, which, they believed, would give them good luck. Superstition or not, they eventually became internationally famous.

Well, What Do You Know?

Mr. F. J. Boase was looking through one of his old books when out fell a 1,000,000 dollar girl bill advertising a musical comedy at the *Hippodrome*. Other advertising for the *Hippodrome*, when a cinema, included the hanging of a dummy outside to advertise the film *All Quiet on the Western Front*.

Twice Nightly

The children's dress would suggest the date as the early 1900s. The *Hippodrome* opened in Princes Street in 1908 as a Music Hall.

In the 1920s it existed not only for live theatre, but also for the showing of films. It opened for sound films on Christmas Day, 1929, with Broadway Melodies. Destroyed by enemy action on the 23rd April, 1941, the site is now the "Red Shield House of the Salvation Army". Devonport people remember its jovial comedians with their loud check suits singing the song of the day, *Have you ever seen a straight banana?"*

Hippodrome Staff of 1931

Back row extreme right: Mr. Ball, foreman of staff. All girls in uniform are usherettes. Two girls wearing dresses without hats were cashiers. Girls recognised are Joan Learwood and Rosie Passmore. Page boys: left, H. J. Watkins. Right: W. Walters. Boys' duties included taking news reels to the Regent Cinema (now Littlewoods) and returning others to the *Hippodrome*.

Hore-Belisha, M.P.

Leslie Hore-Belisha, famous for many things including his "beacons, the posts with yellow globes on top marking street crossing places" is speaking on 29th May, 1929, to a crowd from the *Hippodrome*'s front entrance. He became Devonport's M.P. in 1923, holding Devonport for 22 years, the longest twentieth century hold on the town.

For Whom The Bell Tolls

The chinese coolie hat shaped top of the sixty foot high bell gave the Dockyard policemen some protection from the rain. Used before the introduction of the siren to denote the start and finish of work, the bell was supported on a column behind the imposing wall of the Fore Street South Gate. The column was made from the mainmast of an East Indian Merchantman. The bell came from the French ship, *Tonnant* captured by Nelson at the battle of the Nile. The brass plate on the right hand side of the gate was inscribed: *It is forbidden to take matches into H.M. Dockyard.*

The Hamoaze From Devonport Column

The trees inside the Fore Street South Gate can be seen leading down towards the Terrace. Jimmy Love's Emporium is in the centre of the picture with Catherine Street leading up to Fore Street. A small part of the one mile long limestone Dockyard wall in Edinburgh Row, previously known as Dockwall Street, can be seen on the left a quarter of the way up the picture. Above that again about a third of the way up is the inner wall. Here were the gardens in the rear of the Residences. In the fore ground is the rear of the workmen's dwellings in James Street. Warships, with four funnels, are at anchor in the capacious harbour of the Hamoaze.

The Terrace

Passing down a double row of trees, not far inside the Fore Street Dockyard Gate, stood a fine range of buildings. These fourteen elegant 18th century residences were occupied by the principal officers of the Dockyard. The particularly handsome one belonging to the Admiral Superintendent was approached by two flights of steps. A sole survivor stands after the bombing of 1941. Below the Terrace stood magnificent storehouses and workshops where the highly skilled workers of the Dockyard maintained the ships of the Royal Navy.

Halfpenny Gate, Stonehouse.

Leaving Devonport Behind

The bowler-hatted gentleman having paid his halfpenny toll is on his way to Union Street. Below on his side of the bridge were numerous house-boats and in the water on the other side were many lengths of timber. On the extreme left of the picture was Bluff Battery. Stationed on top of this almost perpendicular broadfront of a cliff was the Second Devon Volunteers of the Artillery Gun Drill Battery. In the left bottom of the picture was a small hospital. Horse-drawn trams would slip off into a bay on the Richmond Walk side of the bridge. Note the wrought iron handwork on the lamp post.

PLYMOUTH'S TOLL GATE
Marjorie Laxton

T'was on the fust of April in 1924,
Us took a trip to Plymouth town,
I'll tell ee now what for.
Us yeard about the freein' of Plymouth's old toll gate,
And 'ow the Mayor was gwaine to be the fust to pass in state.
They told us too that all the schools was 'avin 'oliday,
And that if t'was fine weather, t'would be a fine display.
So up us come that mornin' all feeling bright and gay
For all was lookin' forward to spend a pleasant day.

Well fust of all us took a stroll up on Plymouth Hoe,
But us didn't 'ardly knaw the place for t'was altered so.
Us seed the War Memorial reachin' to the sky,
Or leastways it looked so 'gainst a chap like I.

By then t'was 'lebn o'clock so us come down through the town,
And went into a shop for a feed and a sit down.
Us 'ad tay and pasties and they charged us half a crown,
Us went in with a smile but us come out with a frown,
I said you see the name of that there shop they'm called brown?
I'll see that I dawn't further they next time I comes to town.

Through Union Street us wandered, jest takin' our own time,
Y'eard the church bells ringin' in a merry sort of chime.
All the crowds was cheerin' when us got out on the hill,
So us joined in 'pon me word it did give us a thrill,
To see some men standin' 'oldin' sticks with 'eads of gold,
They was the corporation — or that's what us was told.

Well then us caught sight of the Mayor 'oldin' in 'is 'and
Scissors with which he was to cut the pale blue ribbon band
As soon as he had freed the barrier that barred his way,
Everybody who was there shouted 'ooray 'ooray.
Then all the motor cars come on in endless line,
All the councillors I expect but t'was real fine.

Then there was a bran' new tram car all decorated too,
And charabancs all colours, violet and green and blue,
All in a long procession the children cheered 'em all,
Us loitered there till nothing more could be seen at all
Then us went through the gate to Dem'port for a meal
And all the time the bells continuin' to peal.

Us did enjoy ourselves that day and got home purty late.
For tid'n every day as us can see the freein' of a gate
Besides t'was nearly time for us to 'ave a 'oliday
Us dawn't get nothin' extra 'citin down around our way.
But Plymouth town is smart and bright with many things to see
For folks like us 'tis real joyous or leastways 'tis to me.

Ram the Ram

This was heard by Mr. Pat Ghillyer and others in Cornwall Street, the Workmen's Dwellings in James Street and most places in Devonport each Boxing Day all through the 1920s.

> *Ram the Ram the King of the Jews*
> *Sold his wife for a pair of shoes*
> *And when the shoes began to wear*
> *Ram the Ram began to swear*
> *They hollered him up*
> *They hollered him down*
> *They hollered him all around the town*
> *They knocked him down till he couldn't see*
> *Then fixed him on the holly tree*
> *And there he was as plain could be*
> *Fixed upon the holly tree*
> *A bunch of ribbons by his side*
> *Weeping and wailing for his bride.*

Devonport Central Hall

Wesley Guild Football League Fixture, 1932-33. Standing left to right: N. B. Murray, W. Davies, L. Harris, W. Hocking, G. Clemett, E. Sutton, W. White. Sitting: T. Bennett, H. Robins, R. Watkins, E. Westlake, R. Cousins.

Swimming Award, 1913

The award, bearing Devonport's Arms, was presented to Jack Williams who was a pupil of Stuart Road School. The pupils of this school transferred in the 1950s to Penlee Secondary, whose first headmaster was the forward looking and energetic Mr. H. C. Holding, B.Sc.

One of the instructors in 1913 at the school's swimming lessons held at Mount Wise Old Baths was a Johnny Williams of Torpoint. Jimmy, a relative of Jack, was a coxswain in the Royal Navy, serving the Duke of Edinburgh when he was Commander in Chief at Mount Wise. He taught the Duke's children to swim, including Marie who later became Queen of Rumania.

Somerset Place School, 1938

Back Row: L to R:- Pat Rendle, Margaret Brown, Doris Whitear, Betty Porter, Margaret Miles, ? Joan Salter, Joyce Jeffries, John Brook. 3rd Row: Raymond Haley, Lawrence ? Vivien Wilson, Gordon Perry, Desmond Damerell, Jeffrey Palmer, Joe Rapier, Gordon Spreadborough, Colin Nash, Dennis Sutton, Billy Westlake. 2nd Row: Doreen Horrel, Christine Weeks, Kathleen Pawley, Nesta Naish, Dora Hambly, Heather Jeffries, June Pitcher, Joan Screech, Joan Ross, Joan Webber, Pat Parker. Bottom Row: Roy Pethick, Kenny Morrell, ? Bryant, Alfy Green holding the date 1938, Edward Evans, Norman Lock, Peter Kendall, David Finn.

1907. MORICE TOWN, NORTH CORNER

(including Districts of Keyham, Stoke, and Ford).

REGATTA

To take place off POTTERY QUAY and FERRY BEACH, on

Wednesday, Sept. 11th, commencing 12-30 p.m. sharp.

DONOR:—
H.R.H. The PRINCE OF WALES, K.G., K.P., K.T., &c.

PATRONS:—
Admiral Sir LEWIS A. BEAUMONT, K.C.B., Commander-in-Chief.
Sir JOHN JACKSON, LL.D., F.R.S.
Admiral Supt. C. J. BARLOW, D.S.O.
Commodore FREDERIC E. E. BROCK, A.D.C.
Miss AGNES WESTON.
W. LITTLETON, Esq., J.P.   J. B. JAMES, Esq., J.P.
Capt. J. P. ROLLESTON, R.N.   Capt. CECIL BURNEY, A.D.C., R.N.
Capt. T. L. SHELFORD, R.N.
Capt. and Officers H.M. Torpedo Boat Destroyers. R. DICKESON & Co., Ltd.
WILLIAM MILLER, Ltd.   M. BORG, Esq.
Supt. DIXSON, Metropolitan Police.   J. BUCKLEY, Esq.

Officers:—
President—Alderman Wm. Littleton, J.P.
Chairman—Lieut. F. St. John Boughton, R.N.
Vice-Chairman—Mr. Councillor J. Mayne,   *Starter*—Capt. T. L. Shelford, R.N.
Hon. Treasurer—Mr. C. ACKLAND, Clarence Hotel, Morice Town.
Hon. Secretary—Mr. W. F. BEHENNA, R.N., 8, Ryder Road, Stoke.
Asst. Hon. Secretary—Mr. W. WATSON, 'Prince Arthur' Hotel, Morice Town.
Judges—Mr. W. Sleeman, Mr. J. Mayne, Mr. J. Hellen.
Referee—Mr. H. Kessell.   *Time-keepers*—Mr. F. W. Moreton, Mr. F. E. Norris.
Clerks of Course—Messrs. L. James, Short, R. Green, Connett, H. Baker, Pengelly, Codd, Reed, Jago, J. Sleeman.
Charge of Committee Boats—Messrs. Osborne, Dawe, Broad, R. Behenna, Hearn, Weeks, Feabes, Screech, Rogers, G. Archer.
General Committee—Messrs. J. Hellen, R. G. E. Green, S. Cole, J. Weeks, R. Behenna, W. W. Short, C. J. Hearn, S. C. Reed, F. Codd, S. J. J. Dawe, L. James, A. Sleeman, c.c., R. Pengelly, F. E. Norris, W. H. Osborne, E. Broad, F. Screech, c.c., W. Hellen, A. Williams, H. Kessell, F. Paul, c.c., H. Baker, J. McLaughlan, J. Ellis, W. Littleton, junr., A. Maunder, G. Archer, G. Mellish, J. Connett, R. Sleeman, A. Arscott, L. Paul, G. Mansell, D. Brown, J. Sleep, B. Sercombe, J. Field, J. Feabes, W. Punchas, E. Moon, J. Rogers, G. Pryor, F. W. Moreton, Mus. Bach., J. Wheeler, H. Reep, J. Reep, C. Courteys, and C. Jago.

Perfect Dentistry.

Complete Set of TEETH FROM 15/-

7 Years' Warranty.
No Extraction of Stumps necessary.

18-CARAT Gold Mounted Cases from 2 Guineas.

Teeth Extracted
Absolutely Painless from **1/-**

Nitrous Oxide Gas from 2/6.   Fillings from 2/6.   Gold Fillings from 7/6.

OLD TEETH REPAIRED OR REMODELLED.

Teeth without Plates, Crowns, Bridges, etc.—Our Speciality.

None but the most approved methods in modern Dentistry are employed, and readers are invited to call for advice at their convenience. There is no charge or obligation. If Artificial Teeth are necessary, a definite and extremely moderate price is quoted before the work is commenced.

EXTRACTIONS ARE PAINLESS.

Every English or American method is available, as most suitable to each individual case.

FOWLER & KING'S
DENTAL SURGERY,
31, ALBERT ROAD, DEVONPORT.

DAILY FROM 9 TO 7.

R. H. GIBB, Baker & Confectioner,

32, WILLIAM STREET, MORICE TOWN.

Second Sailing Race—12-50 p.m.

For licensed Watermen's boats, not exceeding 18 feet, with ordinary wood keel, and no outside ballast. (Twice round).

PRIZES:—First, £1.   Second, 15/-.   Third, 7/6.

Name	Color	Entered by
Dream	Blue and White	Foley
White Heather	Blue	Hacker
Lily of Valley	White	J. Higman
Mermaid	Red	W. Foley

Third Sailing Race—1-15 p.m.

For Boats not exceeding 18 feet overall, open to the Port. (Three times round).

PRIZES:—First, Tradesmen's Cup.   Second, £1.   Third, 17/6.   Fourth, 12/6.   Fifth, 7/6.

Name	Color	Entered by
My Lady Dainty	Red and Black Diagonal	T. Hambly
Dorothy	Union Jack	P. Nodder
Frances	Blue and Yellow	J. Reep
Seagull	All Blue	H. Hawkings
Viva	Red and White Diagonal	H. Thompson

R. H. GIBB, Caterer,

Telephone 869.   MORICE TOWN.

R. H. GIBB, Baker & Confectioner,

32, WILLIAM STREET, MORICE TOWN.

Messrs. Bovril, Ltd., will supply their infalliable remedy, i.e., BOVRIL, to all exhausted competitors, free of charge.

First Sailing Race—12-30 p.m.

For Service Cutters, Galleys, Gigs, present pattern service rig and size sails.

Each Competitor to shew a number on each side of the mizen.

Time allowance:—10 seconds per foot, per mile.   Twice round.

PRIZES:—First, £3.   Second, £2.   Third, £1 10s.

Name	Color	Entered by
H.M.S. "Cæsar"—34-ft. Barge	Yellow, Black, Centre either side of Foresail	Lieut. Willcocks
" "Cæsar"—Gig	Yellow and Black	Lieut. G. Cater
" "Andromeda"—30-ft. Cutter	Red 2 o'clock Foresail	Lieut. C. Elwell
" "Niobe"—30-ft. Cutter	White and Red Cross	Lieut. Barkett
" "Niobe"—32-ft. Barge	Do.	Mr. Thompson
" "Niobe"—30-ft. Galley	Do.	G. Hegaty, P.O.
" "Niobe"—27-ft. Whaler	Do.	Jones, C.P.O.
" "Theseus"—No. 2 26-ft. Jolly Boat	Yellow and Blue	E. Pearce, P.O.1.

R. H. GIBB, Caterer,

Telephone 869.   MORICE TOWN.

Morice Town School 1916-17

Harold Feabes, who lived in Gloucester Street, was a pupil of the school, seen here in the third row from bottom and third from left. Also Ron Waller, William Wakely, W. Hendra and Lesley Brown have been recognised. During the last war Miss Betty McAlister, who was a teacher, remembers bombs falling in the Dockyard although no alert had been given. In practically every child's book was a line where they had jumped whilst writing.

The Home Guard Stands Down

In 1940 men enrolled in the Local Defence Volunteers which later became the Home Guard. It became a formidable defence against invasion which, in 1940, seemed to be a certainty. It was stood down in November, 1944, and at the farewell parade on the Hoe on Sunday, 3rd December, 1944, the Lord Mayor expressed the gratitude of the city to those men.

16th Battalion Devonshire Home Guard
"G" Coy. 28a Platoon

STAND DOWN DINNER

At GOODBODY'S CAFE
on November 24th, 1944
at 7 p.m.

The Home Guard at Ease

In this group comprising some members of the 16th Battalion Home Guard, 28th platoon Devonshire G. Coy, are senior private H. Feabes, the Sweet Brothers (shopkeepers), Thomas Damerell, Lieutenant Coombes and Lieutenant Drake. One of the duties was to guard the railway tunnel in the vicinity of the Devonport Technical School.

WARDENS' REPORT FORM.

AIR RAID DAMAGE (Commence with these words).

Date 22 April 1941 Sector No. 1 / G / 9

POSITION OF OCCURRENCE (BLOCK LETTERS) LANGHILL ROAD

TYPE OF BOMB (H.E., ~~I.B., GAS~~ (type if known))   IF UNEXPLODED WRITE "UNX"

CASUALTIES :— Serious Nil   Slight —

NUMBER OF PERSONS TRAPPED :— By Debris —   By Fire —

FIRE. Reported to Auxiliary Fire Station.

Time of Occurrence 1.40 AM   Damage to Mains—WATER / GAS / ELECTRICITY / SEWERS

ROADS BLOCKED   By WRECKAGE / CRATER / FIRE / GAS / UNEXPLODED BOMB

REMARKS and Additional Information :— 16 houses damaged by Blast.

MESSAGE ENDS.

NAME OF WARDEN H. E. Feabes

Air Raid Wardens

The vast proportion were unpaid. Many were decorated for devotion to duty. The Air Raid Precautions (A.R.P.) Wardens' Posts were manned day and night. They were under the charge of a Senior Warden. In dark blue uniforms and gold badges they were called on to perform patrolling duties in the heaviest of raids. Sometimes they would be on duty for five "alerts" in one night. There were, as to be expected in such a hazardous job, casualties among the wardens.

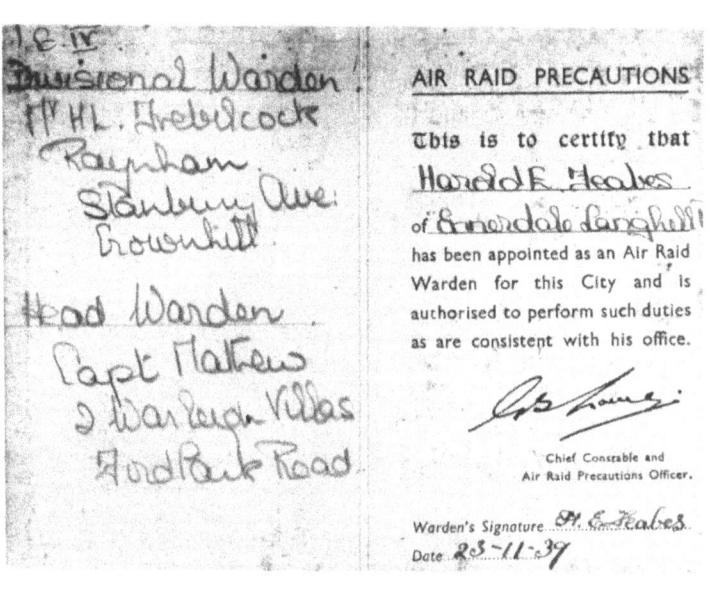

AIR RAID PRECAUTIONS

This is to certify that Harold E. Feabes of Ermendale Langhill has been appointed as an Air Raid Warden for this City and is authorised to perform such duties as are consistent with his office.

Chief Constable and Air Raid Precautions Officer.

Warden's Signature H. E. Feabes
Date 23-11-39

A.R.P. Wardens and Messengers

Harold Feabes is in the back row, sixth from right. On the right is the Curate of St. Gabriel's Church, Reverend J. Ellis. Also in the photograph, which was taken near Trelawny Park Road, Peverell, in Central Park, was Hubert Damerell. Two Civil Defence Messenger boys, who were responsible for keeping communications open between A.R.P. posts during the air raids, are seated on the grass.

Milne Place

Number 5 is seen showing its war scars. All the houses up to number 4, on the right, have been demolished.

Where's The Fire?

The author is using the type of stirrup pump he used during the war. The helmet initials stand for "Street Fire Party".

DEVONPORT 1939-45
G. W. Barker

THE section of the public air-raid shelter in which I had been sitting was full of dust. I found myself lying on the stone floor. As I slowly raised myself the stillness reminded me of the aftermath of an anaesthetic. First, a lone voice was heard, followed by an ever increasing volume of anxious voices. Soon I was able to see the cause of the anxiety. Only a few feet from where I had been sitting I saw that the roof of the shelter was non-existent. It lay in a shattered heap of rubble. I hadn't heard the sound of the bomb, that had hit the corner of the shelter. My younger brother, Lionel, had been playing in the spot where the floor and the roof now merged. Fortunately, he had decided to run down the passage which was at right angles to where I was sitting, seconds before the high explosive landed.

"WAR HAS BEEN DECLARED"

I heard those words from the verger of Saint James the Great Church, as I was leaving the morning service on Sunday, 3rd September, 1939. Soon, together with other eleven year olds, I was helping to fill sandbags for the A.R.P. post at Exmouth Hall at the top of Milne Villas. Later, as a member of the Youth Service Corps I would visit people's houses as one of a squad of four to erect their Morrison table shelters. The shelter comprised in the initial stage a large rectangular sheet of metal with four steel "legs" and a bag full of nuts and bolts. After constructing the shelter in the dining room or the kitchen we would paint the surface. They avoided the necessity of a family having to go out at night to a public air-raid shelter or Anderson shelter in the garden and were safer than sheltering under the stairs.

As the raids increased in intensity so did the amount of shrapnel in the basement at the bottom of our steps in Milne Place. The novelty of saving it wore off with the large quantity that became available. Streets were cordoned off, in the earlier raids, when unexploded bombs were discovered. Later they became so numerous that pedestrians were not prohibited. The Pym Street gang that used to congregate on the corner of Hood Street and Ross Street, looked down the holes in the road left by the UXB's to see if the fins of the bomb could be seen. Even the novelty of seeing a German aircraft shot down with all its markings intact diminished in time. To walk along the path by the side of the present Penlee Secondary School playing fields, in the direction of Central Park, meant one had to pass by a German aircraft. It lay in the field for months.

DEVONPORT ABLAZE

When as a girl of thirteen, Christine Weeks, who is now Mrs. Gardner, remembers walking up Cornwall Street on her way to Fore Street. Air raid wardens, however, were re-directing traffic and people up to where Granby Barracks used to be. No one was allowed to enter Fore Street which had been destroyed. Fires were still burning from the previous night's raid. The smell, she remembered, was terrible and enough to make one choke.

I remember the voice of Mr. Wilks, the air raid warden, calling out above the din of the bombs and guns, when in the public air raid shelter in Devonport Park. He would tell us where the bombs had fallen. One evening he shouted out, "Number five is on fire". We lived in number four and were told that the furniture was being taken out and placed on the pavement across the street. My mother was very philosophical about this; the fact that we were alive was all that mattered she said. We left the shelter after the all clear had sounded. The illuminated white badges that we wore on our coats to assist movement in the blackout were superfluous, owing to the flames that were increasing with the gradual destruction of number five. I helped to fight the fire by working one of the stirrup pumps, but it was a losing battle. A young man who lived at number twelve and whose surname I believe was Bond was walking briskly along the narrow ledge at the top of the houses with buckets of water. Royal Naval volunteer fire fighters from the Barracks gave magnificent assistance and impressed the locals with their professional approach to the danger. The adults on this occasion, as on others during the blitz, taught me how to behave in a crisis.

NEAR MISSES

No matter how many times I heard the air raid siren, and there were 602 "alerts" between July, 1940, when the first bombs were dropped and April, 1944, when the last attack was made, my stomach still "turned over". Through my sleep there was a pause of a couple of seconds, it seemed, between the start of the siren and the monotony of its up and down wailing. During this lull I would hope that I'd been dreaming. The sound of gunfire, however, and drone of the bombers' engines drove us to the shelter across the road. Sometimes the sight had a certain grandeur with searchlights criss-crossing, tracer bullets and flashes filling the sky. Occasionally, after spending a long time in the shelter we would return to our home and be woken soon afterwards by yet another alert. Owing to fatigue, on occasion, we stayed in our beds. After one particularly heavy raid we found that a part of the kerb stone had been lifted into my bedroom by the bomb blast. Long "spears" of glass were protruding from the length of my bed where I had been fast asleep previously before going to the air raid shelter.

Our house escaped destruction from fire owing to the prompt action of Mr. Wilks, the air raid warden, and Mr. Percy Gollop, Special Constable, who had a butcher's shop in Albert Road opposite the *Fellowship* pub. They were patrolling along Pym Street during a heavy raid when they noticed from across the back lane between Milne Place and Hood Street fires burning upstairs in our house. They eventually extinguished the incendiary bombs that would have caused havoc if undetected.

VOLUNTEERS

Mr. Wilks and Percy Gollop were typical of the courageous citizens I saw that saved so many lives and preserved so much property. Mrs. Marian Godden, whose maiden name was Blann, was another air raid warden who faced danger daily. Attached to the same A.R.P. post as Bill Wilks, she patrolled the area with him. She also remembers how after a full day's work in the Dockyard much of his spare time was spent on Civil Defence. He also gave freely of his time as a councillor. The air raid warden's post, under the supervision of Senior Warden William Vercoe, was situated at the top of the park steps at the junction of Ross Street and Milne Place. I have seen Jimmy Rae, the ex-Plymouth Argyle football player, sitting in there. He was a Special Constable.

ENTERTAINMENT

With most of the places of amusement out of action the bombed buildings became a first rate adventure playground. One of Jimmy Rae's tasks was to see that we didn't injure ourselves, though the danger was minimal compared to the nightly air raids. Sometimes we would become air raid "casualties" and lie in the blitzed houses until "rescued" during Civil Defence exercises. On Sunday evenings the Palace Theatre had entertainment for the Armed Forces. In my army cadet uniform, at the age of fourteen, I must have looked the youngest Corporal in the British Army! The seats were occupied by service personnel in a variety of uniforms, including members of the allied forces. During the interval the beautiful voice of June Marlow would be heard. She was too young to appear on stage. Later, Miss Marlow, who worked in Devonport, sang for the Embassy dance band at Milehouse. Eventually she achieved fame with the renowned broadcasters *Stargazers*.

BLAST

The worst experience I had from blast was during the afternoon raid on 25 September, 1940. Pupils of Tamar Central School shared the Johnston Terrace School premises owing to war conditions. One week Tamar Central used the building from eight o'clock to one o'clock and the following week the sessions were reversed, when Tamar pupils attended from one o'clock until five o'clock. On the afternoon of the 25th Dennis Newton, Alan Harper and myself together with other Tamar Central pupils were standing in the concrete surface shelter which stood in the playground. The bombs fell about 4.30 p.m. causing much damage in Goshen and Hamilton Street. The blast whipped into the shelter and was strongly felt by all present. The school itself was later destroyed by enemy action on the night of Monday, 21st April, 1941.

It was not only the air raids which caused casualties. I was walking up the heavily blitzed Gloucester Street, when I saw the body of a boy lying by the side of a static water tank. The tank had been constructed in a bombed house on the corner almost opposite the Salvation Army building. The drowned child had recently been taken out of the water. A tearful relative had arrived on the scene and was talking to the man who had removed the boy.

THE QUEEN'S MESSENGERS

"Lord Haw Haw", whose voice was used for propaganda purposes by the enemy, could be heard clearly on the radio. I would hear the British commentator say, "This is the nine o'clock news", followed by Haw Haw who would say, "Here are the nine o'clock lies". He also forecast that Devonport's turn was to come. The aftermath of the heavy air raids meant all water had to be boiled to avoid contamination. As there were no facilities for cooking hot meals, my mother sent me and my younger brother to get hot soup from the Queen's Messengers. These were well equipped mobile canteens that really moved speedily to areas from London to assist in emergency feeding. The soup was being dispensed from the back of the vans which were standing in Albert Road just below the junction with Charlotte Street.

DEVONPORT REPELS THE INVADERS

I awoke on the Sunday morning to the sound of small arms fire. I had my helmet and armlet on as I cycled up Albert Road on my way to Pounds House in Central Park, which had become the nerve centre of air raid precautions since the original control centres under the Plymouth Guildhall and Devonport Market were burnt out. I had to dodge enemy patrols which had infiltrated past the defences. On arriving at Pounds House I had to put my gas mask on as it had been subjected to a gas attack. Fortunately, it was only tear gas, and the "enemy patrols" were allied servicemen who were taking part in a mock invasion exercise. At the end of the day I stood outside our H.Q., the large house on the corner of Tavistock Road opposite Sherwell Church, and watched the "prisoners" passing. The vehicles had large swastikas chalked on the side and when a motor bike and side car drove by the occupant gave the outstretched Nazi salute. The exercise itself, however, was taken very seriously, as it was the intention that in the event of invasion any attempt to capture Plymouth would be violently opposed. All civilian services were to stand fast. It was expected that the citizens would offer united opposition to the invader and there were clear instructions to be followed.

TRIBUTES

The Western Morning News war correspondent H. P. Twyford on page 18 of his book, *It came to our Door* stated that only a small proportion of the population left the city when danger threatened. Many, he remarked, were driven out because their homes were destroyed and there was no alternative accommodation in the city. He had left instructions in the event of disaster for communal burial with his fellow citizens as he could think of no more honourable ending. Andre Savignon, an exile from invaded France, who shared the ordeals of the blitz, wrote in his book, *With Plymouth Through Fire* that he had never seen the people panic or cry out.

GIFTS FOR THE HUNGRY

Reverend Mansfield, who would often visit the *Gloucester Arms* for a lemonade and a talk with the locals, was the vicar of St. Chads in Moon Street, Morice Town. When I spoke to him at the church after the war he said how gratified he was that the local people, although not well off themselves, gave generously when food parcels were sent to Germany to alleviate their hunger.

A DEVONPORT SHIP

The reality of the war came very early to my family as it did to so many families in Devonport. I remember my mother's anxiety when, in November, 1939, she heard that H.M.S. *Gipsy*, the ship on which Horace, my step-father was serving, had been sunk. H.M.S *Gipsy* had rescued the crew of a German mine-laying aircraft which had come down in the sea. After landing them she once more put to sea, but struck a mine previously laid by the very aircraft whose crew she had saved. Fortunately on arriving at the Royal Naval Barracks she found Horace among the survivors. He also survived the bombing by German planes when on H.M.S. *Illustrious*. After the war an ex-German paratrooper came to live next door. He was of pleasant disposition and well-liked by Horace and our neighbours. Reconciliation had begun.

Where's My Balloon Gone?

The sergeant found that not only had the balloon disappeared, but the heavy lorry as well, to which it was attached by a strong wire. The R.A.F. barrage balloon site was situated on the flat part of Blockhouse complete with nissen hut, near the present toilets. the object of the balloon and wire was to deter enemy aircraft. However, heavy winds had, on this occasion, lifted the lorry like a toy. Luckily for the people in Pasley Street, at the bottom of the hill on the other side of Blockhouse, the lorry's "flight" was arrested half-way down the slope at the rear of the houses in Northesk Street.

Here They Come!

The Devonport Carnival procession passed by the house of Mrs. Husser who lived in Saint Levan's Road before the war. A little way up the hill from Saint Levan Dockyard Gate, approximately where Goshen Yard now stands, the Admiralty, after the war, placed notices stating: "ADMIRALTY PROPERTY KEEP OUT!" Michael Foot, Devonport's M.P., who later became a Freeman of Plymouth protested in Parliament that if the German bombers couldn't drive the people away, why should they. Understanding the local feeling the Admiralty in its wisdom amended the notices to: "Admiralty Property Please Keep Out".

Blockhouse A.R.P. Post

One of the air raid precaution posts still remaining stands in Blockhouse. Outside of it are Mr. Mardy Davies, seated, Mrs. Phyllis Davies, nee Woods, and Mr. Reg. Taylor. Near to the post and adjacent to the present toilets was the public air raid shelter which received a direct hit from a bomb killing many people. Ted Lillicrap of Stoke village and other boys were A.R.P. messengers cycling at the height of the raids carrying messages between various posts.

Bomb Craters

The first alert was on 30th June, 1940. On Saturday 6th July, 1940, shortly before midday under a perfect summer sky, the first enemy bomb came whistling down. It fell on Swilly, (now called North Prospect). A man and boy were killed plus a housewife who had gone back into the house from the garden shelter to look at the dinner that was being cooked. The bomb craters shown on the "Marsh" at Saint Levan's Road were a sample of those that fell in the area. In three raids on 12th July, 1940, several bombs were dropped in Saint Levan's and Alma Road areas.

Night Time Raid

The picture looking across Saint Levan's Road from the "Marsh" was taken in the glare of flares and gun flashes at night. On Monday 8th July, 1940, during the third raid in which bombs were dropped, four fell in the vicinity of Morice Square. A butcher's shop in Marlborough Street, near the Devonport Hospital, received a direct hit. Mr. Slee, the proprietor was killed. Another bomb went straight through the Royal Sailors' Club in Morice Square exploding in the kitchen destroying the dining room. Half an hour previously it had been crowded with sailors having their breakfast before going aboard their ships.

War Damage

Rubble from bomb damage is strewn across Alexandra Road in Ford. Gardens in many houses were equipped with the sturdy Anderson Shelters. Street after street of once pleasant homes were shattered by the enemy's bombs. The whole area would shake with the intense bombardment. At night large fires lit the sky. Shops that had been devastated carried on business as usual with a typical slogan chalked, "More Open Than Ever"!

Portland Place

A low raider in the moonlight on 10th January, 1941, dropped a large bomb at the junction of Portland Place and Charlotte Street, by the steps in Devonport Park. It was probably intended for the nearby Dockyard. The author remembers walking down Milne Place past the ornate looking house in Ross Street, and along Gloucester Street. Walking up the hill of Charlotte Street he saw a victim lying in the gutter being covered by a sheet held by rescue workers.

A Gallant Ally

The girls from the orphanage in Albert Road were evacuated to Truro. The building now echoed with the footsteps of the Polish sailors who were well liked by the people of Devonport. Three Polish destroyers; *Grom, Burza* and *Blyskevica* and later the submarines *Wilk* and *Orzel* (the latter escaping from interment in Estonia) were with us in the war's early days. The author, as a boy, remembers the welcome given to local children to see musicals like, "The Chocolate Soldier" at their film shows. The plaque to the memory of the Polish Navy is erected outside the Naval Base entrance in Albert Road.

1945 Victory Street Party

This party was at Cambridge Road, Ford. Sometimes the long wooden benches were obtained from the air raid shelters and used by the children for seating. The author particularly remembers the party in Pym Street, where a piano was strategically placed opposite the corner pub. Music and dancing was the theme at these Victory celebrations.

The Post Office in 1903

The post office in Fore Street was a magnificent building. The rotunda columns with the entablature above were copied from the Temple of Tivoli. The building was adorned with; symbols of postal despatch, produce of England, and the pride of Devonport as a military and naval arsenal. The building, with its elegant semi-circular portico, was erected in 1849. Devonport was connected with Stonehouse and Plymouth by Electric Tramways (Green Cars). One of them is waiting to go, and they ran every two or three minutes.

Samuel Phelps

He was born in St. Aubyn Street in 1804. He became a famous actor. When seventeen he walked to London. Without his enthusiasm Saddlers Wells might not have been the famous institution it has become. During his twenty years there he was instrumental in making it one of the foremost theatres in London. He would have been proud to know that Wayne Sleep, of the Royal Ballet, who was born in Plymouth, has become one of the greatest dancers in Great Britain.

J. C. Tozer

Ten minutes tram ride from North Road Station. Ten minutes walk from Devonport G.W.R. Station. Eight minutes walk from Devonport Southern Station. Before the 1939 war the store for the greatest value in furniture had a Jacobean dining room suite for £4.10s. (four pounds ten shillings). A four foot sideboard solidly built of grained oak finish was thirty shillings.

Pembroke Street Butcher

Mr. George Bickle, who later became the owner of this shop in Pembroke Street, which was near the Baptist Church, is the elder gentleman on the right. He worked from 4 a.m., till 11 p.m., on Saturday nights when the joints were sold cheaply. He was a Steward at Devonport Methodist Central Hall. During the 1914-1918 war he was a Special Constable, being attached to the police station at Ker Street. When blitzed from his shop in the 1939-45 war he had a butchers shop opposite the *Kings Arms* in Pembroke Street. During the war, although over 70, he would work at the slaughter house, near Devonport Market, on his Wednesday half day holiday, because of the shortage of men.

The Pembroke Street Baptist Church

The interior of the church is clearly seen. Records go back to 1779, when a meeting house in Liberty Street (later to be called Pembroke Street), was used to accommodate worshippers. They had previously travelled to Plymouth where a Reverend Philip Gibbs was the pastor of a meeting house in the pig market. One of the first ministers of the church was Rev. Isaiah Birt. In 1954 notice was served for demolition and the organ and pulpit were incorporated in the new building at Crownhill. Some members of the congregation, like the popular brothers Norman and Jack Head, shared in the worship at Devonport Methodist Central Hall.

Stand And Deliver

The sunshade belongs to the post office at the corner of James Street and Pembroke Street. Sammy Clarke, who became a Devonport Councillor, is holding the reins of the horse and dray. The driver is Taff Williams. The post office was a hive of industry, where many sailors would walk up from the Mutton Cove area, having returned from two or three years abroad. Some would send a post card home before spending much of their hard-earned money in the numerous pubs in Pembroke Street.

Alex Ash and Son

Mr. Jack Williams worked for this firm in the 1920s. Deliveries of wine and beer were undertaken for many years by horse. The building was situated on the right of the post office in James Street. Not far away on the corner of St. Stephens Lane, there was a lovely dairy run by Viggers. Mrs. M. Laxton remembers one could get a large white jug full of milk for one penny.

China Town

Here in the 1920s Pembroke Street is decorated for the carnival. It was nicknamed *China Town*. It was a densely populated area with an abundance of small shops. The author lived at 16 Fort Street, in the early 1930s. It was one of the many side streets that intersected Pembroke Street. The children downstairs at number 16 slept on bare floorboards, with skimpy coverings. Although unemployment meant there was little money about, water was plentiful and the youngsters were clean and of cheerful disposition.

Hello Sailors

One of the names on the sailors' hat bands was *Vivid*. The Royal Navy Barracks which are north of the North Yard of the Naval Base were rated at one time as a ship named, H.M.S. *Vivid*. The barracks were used as a Depot for seamen and stokers. The buildings were commenced in 1879 and completed in 1886.

Dive! Dive! Dive!

Chief Engine Room Artificer Arthur Barker, the author's brother, was typical of the submariners who never spoke of the dangers inherent in their job. When Winston Churchill died, he was invited to attend the funeral. A newspaper cutting stated, "Arthur C. Barker will take his place today among members of Royalty, Heads of State, Senior Officers and friends who will crowd Saint Paul's Cathedral to pay their last respects to Winston Churchill. He is a Chief Engineer in the Merchant Navy. He was in the Royal Navy for 16 years, serving on submarines during the Second World War, and is now a Lieutenant (Engineer) in the Royal Naval Reserve."

On Sea and Land

The Royal Navy was not only involved in keeping the peace at sea. During the Great War 1914-18 a Royal Naval Brigade fought in the trenches in France. In the early 1950s the author remembers leaving the R.N. Barracks with the ships's company to join H.M.S. *Flamingo* in the Persian Gulf. One of the Navy's tasks was to stop the traffic of slaves in the area.

Stand And Deliver

The sunshade belongs to the post office at the corner of James Street and Pembroke Street. Sammy Clarke, who became a Devonport Councillor, is holding the reins of the horse and dray. The driver is Taff Williams. The post office was a hive of industry, where many sailors would walk up from the Mutton Cove area, having returned from two or three years abroad. Some would send a post card home before spending much of their hard-earned money in the numerous pubs in Pembroke Street.

Alex Ash and Son

Mr. Jack Williams worked for this firm in the 1920s. Deliveries of wine and beer were undertaken for many years by horse. The building was situated on the right of the post office in James Street. Not far away on the corner of St. Stephens Lane, there was a lovely dairy run by Viggers. Mrs. M. Laxton remembers one could get a large white jug full of milk for one penny.

China Town

Here in the 1920s Pembroke Street is decorated for the carnival. It was nicknamed *China Town*. It was a densely populated area with an abundance of small shops. The author lived at 16 Fort Street, in the early 1930s. It was one of the many side streets that intersected Pembroke Street. The children downstairs at number 16 slept on bare floorboards, with skimpy coverings. Although unemployment meant there was little money about, water was plentiful and the youngsters were clean and of cheerful disposition.

Hello Sailors

One of the names on the sailors' hat bands was *Vivid*. The Royal Navy Barracks which are north of the North Yard of the Naval Base were rated at one time as a ship named, H.M.S. *Vivid*. The barracks were used as a Depot for seamen and stokers. The buildings were commenced in 1879 and completed in 1886.

Dive! Dive! Dive!

Chief Engine Room Artificer Arthur Barker, the author's brother, was typical of the submariners who never spoke of the dangers inherent in their job. When Winston Churchill died, he was invited to attend the funeral. A newspaper cutting stated, "Arthur C. Barker will take his place today among members of Royalty, Heads of State, Senior Officers and friends who will crowd Saint Paul's Cathedral to pay their last respects to Winston Churchill. He is a Chief Engineer in the Merchant Navy. He was in the Royal Navy for 16 years, serving on submarines during the Second World War, and is now a Lieutenant (Engineer) in the Royal Naval Reserve."

On Sea and Land

The Royal Navy was not only involved in keeping the peace at sea. During the Great War 1914-18 a Royal Naval Brigade fought in the trenches in France. In the early 1950s the author remembers leaving the R.N. Barracks with the ships's company to join H.M.S. *Flamingo* in the Persian Gulf. One of the Navy's tasks was to stop the traffic of slaves in the area.

Happy Go-Lucky Sailors

Submariners wearing their white polo-necked jumpers, and relaxing during brief periods of leisure at 4 Milne Place during the 1939-45 war impressed the author with their "happy-go-lucky" ways. Tragedy, however, would often strike these submariners who approached their jobs so professionally. The submarine A8 left for exercises on the fateful day of 8th June 1905. She sank and 15 of her crew were drowned. Launched at the Naval Construction Works in Barrow on 23rd January, 1905, she was on her way to Looe when there was an underwater explosion.

Submarine Cross

The cross was made from a piece of the metal from the plate that was removed from the submarine to give access to the bodies. The A8 was raised and placed in the Devonport Dockyard, where the plate was removed. The cross was made by a Mr. Pinch. It is 3 inches high. Mrs. N. Pollard (who loaned the photograph) said her Grandmother, who worked in the Ropery in South Dockyard, was given two hours off to go to the Chapel for the service for the submariners. She died aged 40 owing to the breathing of oakum, there being no means of extracting the air at her place of work.

Full Honours

The funeral procession of the victims of the submarine A8 disaster passing Stoke Damerel Church. The men spectators bare their heads, as the coffins pass. The corporal, in the foreground, comes to the salute, and the soldiers lining the route have their arms reversed. Straw hats are still worn by the sailors in 1905.

Outside Devonport Guildhall 1924

At the Bazaar, held in the Guildhall was Mrs. J. R. Gribbell's mother in furs, Mrs. Baldwin and the Marquin family. Devonport Guildhall was the scene of many political campaigns. Devonport in the last fifty years has had only four M.P.s and each one of them has made their mark. Leslie Hore-Belisha, Liberal National (1923), later to become Chamberlain's Secretary of State for War in 1939. Michael Foot, Labour, (1945) became leader of the Labour Party. Miss Joan Vickers, Conservative (1955), Dame of the British Empire in 1964 and as Baroness Vickers of Devonport she was granted the Freedom of Plymouth in 1982, acknowledging service to Plymouth and Devonport in both Houses of Parliament. Dr. David Owen, Labour (1974) became Navy Minister, Health Minister and at 38 the youngest Foreign Secretary apart from Anthony Eden. He is now the leader of the Social Democratic Party.

Wedding Group, 1st October, 1924

This was the kind of occasion at which Sibley's would excel. A wedding reception, one of the first being held in the building, is taking place at the Cumberland Assembly Rooms, which was off Cumberland Street, near the Devonport market. The reception is that of Mr. and Mrs. Leonard Baldwin. Members of the Baldwin and Voss families were also present.

Arthur L. Clamp – the man behind the books

Arthur Leslie Clamp was a man of boundless energy with a passion for helping others, particularly through his love of history. A printer by trade, he started his career in a printing company before moving his family from Exeter to Plymouth to teach at the Plymouth College of Art and Design, where he eventually became the Head of the Printing Department.

A Devoted Family Man

Arthur with his five children.

Despite his love of teaching, Arthur prioritised his family, always making it home by 5:30pm for tea. He and his wife, Rosemary, raised five children: Susan, Angela, Elizabeth, David, and Steven. Arthur would often combine his love of family and history by taking his children on Sunday walks, encouraging them to appreciate historical monuments by taking photos or making crayon rubbings of gravestones for his books. The family home at 203 Elburton Road was a hub of activity, with a large garden, featuring a two-storey fort and a makeshift swimming pool.

A Lifelong Learner and Adventurer

Arthur's thirst for knowledge extended beyond history to a deep curiosity about the world. He was passionate about exploring different cultures, traditions, and cuisines, often taking advantage of his long summer holidays as a teacher to travel to places like India, Russia, South America, the middle east and the USA, sometimes bringing one of his children along. This adventurous spirit even influenced his home life, as seen by the short-lived family tradition of steam-cooking vegetables after a trip to Iceland.

History is a prominent feature of family days out

Community and Philanthropic Spirit

His commitment to serving others was evident in his long-standing involvement with the Elburton Methodist Church. He was the Sunday School Superintendent for over 15 years and served as the editor of the wider church's monthly newsletter, "The Link," for a similar duration. After Rosemary's very sad passing, Arthur later remarried and, following a chance encounter with a professor from India, established a connection with a missionary school in Chennai. Together with his new wife, Christine, he co-founded a "Sponsor a Child's Education" program that continues to this day.

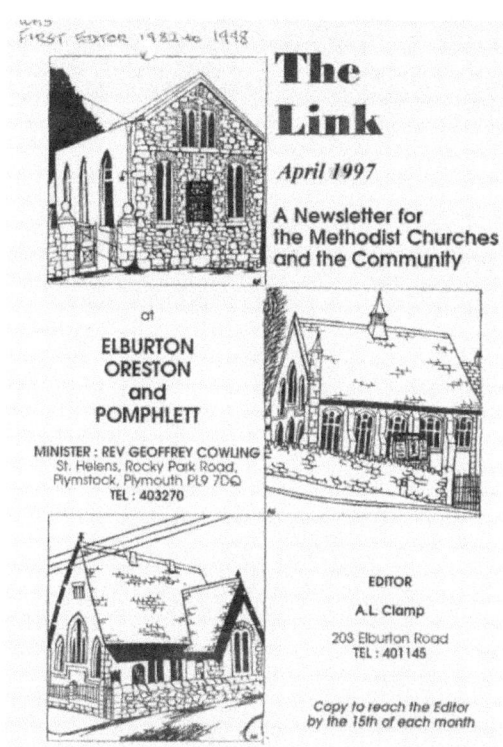

*Pictured left – The cover of 'The Link' complete
with hand drawn sketches of each church by Angela
Below right – Arthur Clamp promoting his latest book
Below left – Arthur at home with his first wife, Rosemary
Below centre – Arthur on holiday with his second wife, Christine*

A Legacy of Learning and Positivity

Arthur's greatest passion was history, which he brought to life through tireless research, documentation, and the many books he authored. He was driven by a need to "never be stuck in a rut," constantly seeking new experiences, meeting new people, and expanding his knowledge. With a positive attitude and a great sense of humour, he was always ready to help others, leaving a lasting impact on his family and community. His children, Susan, Angela, Elizabeth, David, and Steven, remember him with love and gratitude.

David Clamp, 2025

A Legacy of Local History

Below is the story of how Arthur L Clamp began writing books, in his own words, drafted shortly before he passed away in 2001. I have only made minor alterations to this text, correcting grammatical errors that he did not survive to correct himself. When I first discovered this text, I was shocked to see my name mentioned. It seems that, unbeknownst to me, I shared my first PC with him. I suspect he used it during the day when I was at school, although I do have one memory of sitting with him and showing him how it worked. It has been a pleasure to pick up where he left off and see his books republished and redistributed, and to know that I was part of the story, even back then. It was also fascinating to discover that his pricing structure matches the way I have tried to price the books, with a third going to local sellers and the rest covering printing costs with a little left over for my expenses.

I am his eldest grandson, and it is a privilege to curate his legacy, which we are calling 'The Clamp Collection'. The very last line of the text originally reads "The following pages list all the titles." Sadly, that page is missing and we have no record of all the books he published and knowing that some of those were researched by other authors makes the process of finding them even harder. I look forward to one day completing the collection and seeing them all available again. And maybe, one day, I'll even start writing my own to add to the series. For now, here is his story in his own words.

Steven Gibson, 2025

Writing and Publishing Booklets on Local Topics and Areas

I started this interest in either 1968 or 1969 when living in Woodford. I had by these dates established the Department of Printing and I think I must have been looking for something different to do. The first titles were of A5 size proofed from type set at Clarke, Doble and Brendon, Ltd., Plymouth printers, and then made up into pages and printed at Sawtell and Neilson, Ltd., Totnes.

Then began a slow process of getting them out to shops, etc. which proved to be more time consuming and difficult than actually researching, writing and getting the books into print. However, I persisted and opened a business account with Barclays Bank on the Broadway. I was advised to give it a title so I called it "Westway Publications". There came along another problem, one of storage of paper and finished books which was solved when the family moved to Elburton in 1970.

I changed the printer to Penwell, Ltd., Callington, Cornwall, as he was then just setting up himself and his prices seemed very reasonable. I did not get any of the printers to make up the complete books. I hand folded the flat printed sheets, stitched the books on a small manual table stitcher and trimmed them in a small hand turned guillotine which I bought from someone in Penzance for £40. It was brought up in a van.

The trouble and time going to and fro to Callington was too much so I transferred the printing to PDS Printers, Prince Rock, Plymouth, and I have been with them ever since. Now they are at Plympton which is easy to reach and they fold the flat sheets which was turning out to be a long chore which only saved a small part of the printing costs.

All my first titles were written by myself. I took the photographs and developed them in the loft of the house, the type was set by now on a computer situated in the house at Elburton from which I had collected photographic lengths of text to cut up and law down as pages.

At some point I decided that I would do my own film processing of lith film so I bought a large second hand process camera from Kingsbridge and learnt through trial and error to make line negatives of the text and halftone negatives of the illustrations which proved more difficult than I anticipated. The main problem was trying to keep the developer in the large dish at the correct temperature as any change would affect the developing time. I replaced this old camera with a brand new one bought from Croydon, Surrey, costing £900. This has turned out to be a great asset cutting out an expensive part of the printer's costs and one crucial aspect of the work which I could control.

By the middle 1970s there were many outlets I had contacted in Plymouth, up to Dartmoor, Exeter, around to Torbay, Totnes, Dartmouth and the South Hams. The market for local books was much greater than I had first thought and through getting to know many local people undertaking research themselves had the chance to help and make up books for other people who had in most instances, got together a collection of photographs with some text in a rather muddled way. Through my experience in print I was able to shape up their work and get it into print and in every case I had to pay the printer and let the person have the royalties. In the majority of titles produced in this manner this was another way of producing titles and it did give some profit to my work. However, I must say that in a few cases I lost out by either the other person getting the numbers wrong, not returning any monies from stock I delivered or they thought that more of their books should have been sold.

The print run was usually 1,000 copies and from time to time I have had reprints of 250 copies. It took about ten years to clear the first print run so I always had large stocks in the garage, workshop, etc. The numbers sold during the early years was about 7,000 copies a year increasing to around 9,000 copies and for the whole of the enterprise about 500,000 have been sold. The booklets have become part of the local scene and many people collect them, shops regularly order copies and I go around certain areas month by month restocking or replacing titles as necessary.

During the past year or so I have started setting the text on a Packard Bell PC, something which I should have done some years back. I share it with Steven Gibson, my grandson. There appears to be no end to the market for local books, but I could not earn a regular income because of the long time it takes to sell stock.

However, now exceeding 100 titles made up mainly of A4 twenty-four page booklets, some folded guides, with selling prices set with a third going to the shop which is the trade custom, the original idea has been quite successful and could go on for ever.

Apart from monetary benefits, however spasmodically these might be, I have learnt a lot myself, met many interesting people and have become part of the local scene with requests to give talks and to advise people about getting into print.

Arthur L Clamp, 2001

Death of local historical author

'He was an incredible character who was just loved by everybody who knew him'

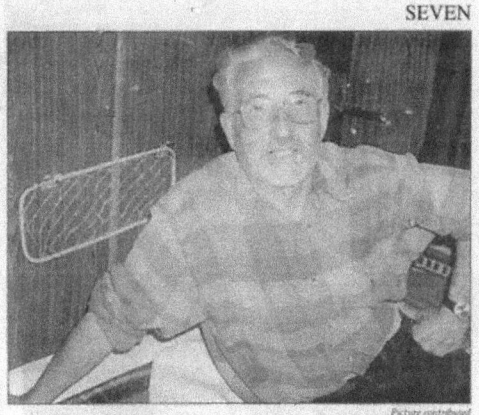

A WELL-loved Elburton author has died at the age of 68.

Arthur Clamp (pictured right), who was one of the West Country's most successful writers, died at St Luke's Hospice, Turnchapel, after losing his battle against cancer.

Tributes have been flooding in for a man who was known in the community as a prominent writer and outgoing person.

He produced more than 140 titles during his life, dealing with both fiction, fact and history, often discussing West Country topics that were close to his heart.

One of his most acclaimed books was *The Plymouth Blitz*, and he also won credit for *The Rise and Fall of the Bearings of Membland Hall*, set in Noss Mayo.

He achieved sales of between 7,000 and 9,000 books every year and it is estimated that he has sold over half a million books, covering the areas of Plymouth, Dartmoor, Exeter, Torbay and the South Hams.

Mr Clamp was born in Mitcham, Surrey, in 1932, and was the eldest of four children.

He moved to Devon in 1941 to avoid the London air-raids.

Mr Clamp trained as a printer in Exeter and also gained a teachers' certificate in 1959 from Garnet College in London.

Plymouth College of Art, however, was to prove to be Mr Clamp's working home for the following 32 years until 1991, when he retired as head of the printing department.

He had a great interest in travel and had visited the USA, Tanzania, China, Russia, Peru, as well as travelling across Europe, where he presented talks and slide shows on his experiences as a writer.

Mr Clamp was a member of Elburton Methodist Church for many years, superintendent of the Sunday school and editor of the church newsletter, as well as being involved in much charity work.

He was president of the Plymouth and District Field Club and an active member of the Elburton Residents' Association.

He enjoyed leading walks on Dartmoor and historical tours throughout the West Country.

Mr Clamp married his first wife, Rosemary, in 1956 and they had five children - Susan, Angela, Elizabeth, David and Steven - and she died in 1987. He also had 11 grandchildren.

He leaves a wife Christine, after remarrying in 1991, and her two children and three grandchildren.

'He was an incredible character who was just loved by everybody who knew him,' said his wife.

'He will be missed by his family, his friends, the people he worked with and just everybody who knew him through his books.'

More than 300 mourners attended his funeral at Elburton Methodist Church on Monday.

'The attendance was a celebration of his life - he would have found that really special. It shows his vibrancy and love of people,' said Mrs Clamp.

Steven Clamp added that his father was 'a well respected and loved man, missed by a great many people throughout the South West and far beyond'.

This newspaper article, published by the Evening Herald on 17th August 2001, forms a good record of his life. Just as he encourages us to learn more about local history, we encourage you to learn a little about him. For that reason, we have included these pages at the back of all the most recently republished books, in honour of his memory and recognition of his contribution to the community.

www.ingramcontent.com/pod-product-compliance
Lightning Source LLC
Chambersburg PA
CBHW061407070526
44584CB00031B/4180